KU-351-560

Why do we remember?

NEIL ARMSTRONG AND THE MOON LANDINGS

Izzi Howell

PROPERTY OF MERTHYR
TYDFIL PUBLIC LIBRARIES

Franklin Watts
Published in Great Britain in paperback in 2018 by The Watts Publishing Group
Copyright © The Watts Publishing Group, 2016

 Produced for Franklin Watts by
White-Thomson Publishing Ltd
www.wtpub.co.uk

All rights reserved.

ISBN: 978 1 4451 4843 4

Credits
Series Editor: Izzi Howell
Series Designer: Rocket Design (East Anglia) Ltd

The publisher would like to thank the following for permission to reproduce their pictures:
Alamy/Tor Eigeland p21 (bottom); Corbis/John Aikins - The Stock Connecti/Science Faction
15; iStock/CSA-Images 8, iStock/Purdue9394 28; NASA cover, 2, 3, 4 (top), 5, 7, 10, 11, 12,
13, 16, 17 (top), 17 (bottom), 18, 19, 20 (left), 20 (right), 22, 23 (bottom), 24, 25; NASA/
Bill Ingalls 29; NASA/David Scott 3, 26; NASA/Les Bossinas (Cortez III Service Corp) 27;
NASA/Mitch Ames23 (top), NASA/Science Photo Library 9; Stefan Chabluk 14; Shutterstock/
Christos Georghiou cover, Shutterstock/HelenField 4 (bottom), Shutterstock/Knumina Studios 6,
Shutterstock/Nicholas Greenaway cover, Shutterstock/Quaoar 21 (bottom).
All design elements from Shutterstock.

Every attempt has been made to clear copyright. Should there be any inadvertent omission
please apply to the publisher for rectification.

Printed in China

MIX
Paper from
responsible sources
FSC® C104740
www.fsc.org

Franklin Watts
An imprint of
Hachette Children's Group
Part of The Watts Publishing Group
Carmelite House
50 Victoria Embankment
London EC4Y 0DZ

An Hachette UK Company
www.hachette.co.uk
www.franklinwatts.co.uk

Words in **bold** can be found in the glossary on p30.

" One small step for a man, one giant leap for mankind. "
Neil Armstrong

CONTENTS

WHO WAS NEIL ARMSTRONG?

Neil Armstrong was the first man to walk on the Moon. This was an important moment in history, as no human had ever landed on an object in space before.

On 20 July 1969, Armstrong, and another astronaut named Buzz Aldrin, landed on the surface of the Moon in the *Eagle* **lunar module**. Millions of people around the world watched on TV as Armstrong took the first steps on the Moon.

▶ The *Eagle* lunar module came down to land on the Moon's surface.

66 Houston. **Tranquillity Base** here. The *Eagle* has landed. 99

Neil Armstrong

HOW do we know?

We can listen to **interviews** with Neil Armstrong to hear the story of the Moon landing in his own words.

▶ In this photo, Neil Armstrong is wearing the spacesuit that he wore on the Moon.

LEARNING TO <u>FLY</u>

Neil Armstrong was born in Ohio, USA, in 1930. As a child, Neil was interested in aeroplanes. He built model **aircraft** and read magazines about flying. He got his pilot's license when he was 16 and started flying planes by himself.

At university, Neil studied how planes fly. He trained to be a pilot with the US Navy and flew **fighter planes** during the **Korean War**. At the age of 25, he got a job working for the National Aeronautics and Space Administration (**NASA**) as a **test pilot**.

▼ When he was five or six, Neil Armstrong went up in an aeroplane for the first time. The aeroplane would have looked similar to this one.

Hi mum!

◄ In his job at NASA, Neil tried out new aeroplanes to make sure they were flying properly.

WHAT do you think?

This photo of Neil Armstrong as a test pilot was taken a long time ago. How can you tell?

FIND OUT FOR YOURSELF
In which town in Ohio was Neil Armstrong born?

THE SPACE RACE

Neil Armstrong worked at NASA during the exciting **Space Race** of the 1950s and 1960s. The Space Race was a competition between the USA and the **Soviet Union**, which later became Russia. Both countries wanted to be the first to send a man into space, and eventually, to land on the Moon.

▼ At the time of the Space Race, many comic books and TV programmes showed incredible imaginary scenes from space.

In 1961, the Soviet Union jumped into the lead when they sent a man into space for the first time. Yuri Gagarin **orbited** the Earth once in his spacecraft, *Vostok 1*, before coming safely back down.

▶ A US newspaper from 12 April 1961 – the day that Yuri Gagarin went into space.

The Huntsville Times

Man Enters Space

'So Close, Yet So Far,' Sighs Cape

U.S. Had Hoped For Own Launch

Soviet Officer Orbits Globe In 5-Ton Ship

Maximum Height Reached Reported As 188 Miles

Praise Is Heaped On Major Gagarin

First Man To Enter Space Is 27, Married, Father Of Two

VON BRAUN'S REACTION:

To Keep Up, U. S. A. Must Run Like Hell

Reds Win Running Lead In Race To Control Space

<u>HOW</u> do we know?

We can look at newspapers from the time, and see headlines about Yuri Gagarin's trip to space.

FIND OUT FOR YOURSELF
Which country did the first woman in space come from?

PROJECT GEMINI

The Soviet Union had sent the first man into space, but the Space Race was far from over. In 1962, NASA started a new space exploration project – Project Gemini. On the *Gemini* flights, astronauts went into space and practised the skills that they would need for a Moon landing.

In 1966, NASA chose Neil Armstrong to be the **command pilot** on the *Gemini 8* flight. *Gemini 8* made it into space, but it had to return to Earth early because it had problems after joining up with another spacecraft.

◄ In this photo, Neil Armstrong (front) is about to **board** the *Gemini 8* spacecraft. This was his first trip into space.

HOW do we know?

We can see photos of astronauts practising new skills on *Gemini* flights, such as **spacewalks**.

▼ On the *Gemini 4* flight, an astronaut left the spacecraft and walked in space for the first time.

oh look, there's my house!

WHAT do you think?

What do you think a spacewalk would feel like?

PROJECT APOLLO

After ten **manned** *Gemini* flights, NASA was ready to plan a Moon landing. They designed a new type of spacecraft that could land on the Moon. They called this spacecraft *Apollo*.

NASA sent astronauts on test flights in the *Apollo* spacecraft to make sure it worked properly. They chose *Apollo 11* as the flight that would land on the Moon.

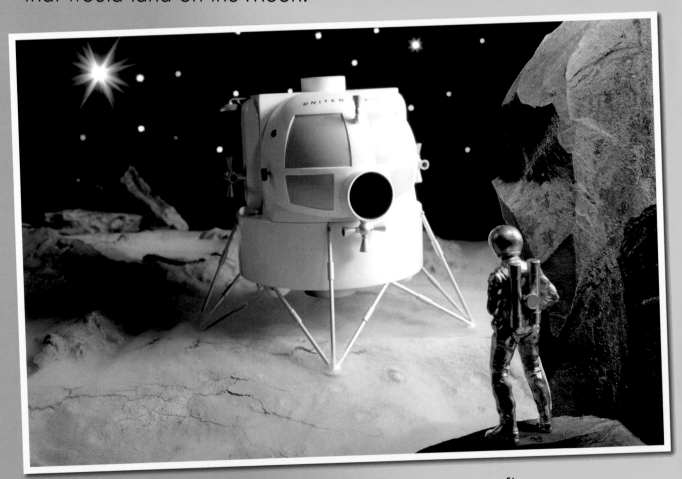

▲ This is a model of a Moon landing spacecraft. NASA made models before building a full-sized spacecraft to see which design worked best.

> 66 It suddenly struck me that that tiny pea, pretty and blue, was the Earth ... I felt very, very small. 99
>
> Neil Armstrong

▲ Astronauts on the *Apollo* flights took photographs of the Earth from space.

WHAT do you think?

It's hard to imagine how big the Earth is. How have your ideas about the size of the Earth changed after looking at this photo?

SUPER SPACECRAFT

The *Apollo* spacecraft had three different parts. The three *Apollo 11* astronauts travelled into space in the **command module**, which was powered by rockets kept inside the **service module**. The lunar module was used for landing on the Moon.

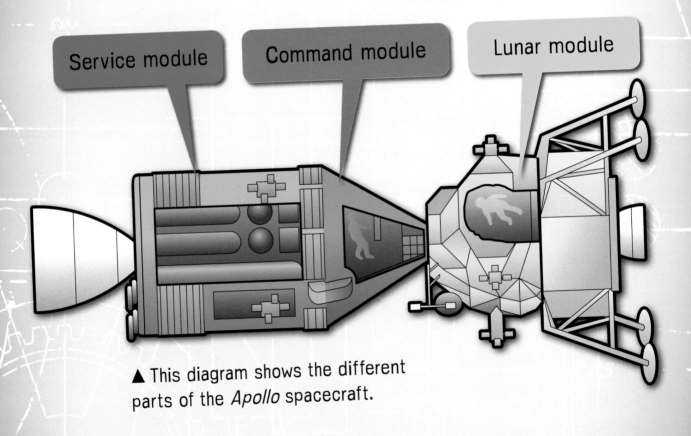

Service module

Command module

Lunar module

▲ This diagram shows the different parts of the *Apollo* spacecraft.

A powerful rocket called *Saturn V* would blast *Apollo 11* into space. At the time, *Saturn V* was the tallest, heaviest and most powerful rocket ever created.

HOW do we know?

You can visit the command module at the National Air and Space Museum in the USA. The lunar and service modules were left behind in space, as it would have been hard to bring them back to Earth.

▼ The inside of the command module is about the same size as the inside of a large car.

WHAT do you think?

What things would the astronauts have needed inside the command module to help them live in space?

PROPERTY OF MERTHYR TYDFIL PUBLIC LIBRARIES

MEET THE CREW

NASA chose three **experienced** astronauts as the crew of *Apollo 11* – Neil Armstrong, Edwin (Buzz) Aldrin and Michael Collins. All three astronauts had been into space before on *Gemini* flights.

Neil Armstrong was in charge of the **mission**. Buzz Aldrin was the pilot of the lunar module and Michael Collins was the command module pilot.

▼ This photo of the *Apollo 11* crew was taken before their trip to the Moon.
(left to right Armstrong, Collins, Aldrin)

APOLLO 11

◀ The *Apollo 11* crew wore this mission badge on their uniforms.

These space boots weigh a ton!

▲ Armstrong and Aldrin practised moving in their spacesuits as part of their training.

WHAT do you think?

What sort of person do you think would make a good astronaut?

FIND OUT FOR YOURSELF
Which Apollo 11 astronaut designed the mission badge?

BLAST <u>OFF</u>!

On 16 July 1969, crowds gathered at the Kennedy Space Center in Florida, USA, to watch the launch of *Apollo 11*. At 9.32 a.m., the *Saturn V* rocket was fired. *Apollo 11* and its crew were blasted into space.

As the *Apollo 11* spacecraft flew further away from the Earth, the *Saturn V* rocket fell away, landing in the ocean. *Apollo 11* continued on its journey. Three days later, it began to orbit the Moon.

▶ After take-off, *Apollo 11* reached a speed of nearly 39,000 kilometres per hour.

HOW do we know?

People all over the world watched the launch of *Apollo 11* on TV. There were also many **eyewitnesses**, as people came to the Kennedy Space Center to watch it blast off.

WHAT do you think?

Have you been an eyewitness to any important events? How is seeing an event different to hearing about it from other people?

▲ Crowds of people, including the former president of the USA, Lyndon B. Johnson (centre), watched the *Apollo 11* launch.

A <u>BIG</u> STEP

After four days in space, the *Apollo 11* crew prepared for landing. While Collins orbited the Moon alone in the command module, Armstrong and Aldrin travelled down to the Moon's surface in the lunar module.

Neil Armstrong was the first astronaut to step out of the spacecraft onto the dusty surface of the Moon. His first steps on the Moon were **broadcast** live to around 600 million TV viewers.

◀ Minutes after his first steps on the Moon, Armstrong took this photo of Aldrin.

▼ Armstrong's footprint on the Moon's surface.

HOW do we know?

You can watch a video of the Moon landing on NASA's website and listen to Armstrong's famous words as he stepped onto the Moon.

> " One small step for a man, one giant leap for mankind. "
>
> Neil Armstrong

▶ People around the world tuned in to watch the Moon landing live on TV.

WHAT do you think?

Why do you think so many people watched the Moon landing on TV?

PROPERTY OF MERTHYR TYDFIL PUBLIC LIBRARIES

WALKING ON THE MOON

There is no air on the Moon. The astronauts wore helmets with **oxygen** inside and spacesuits to protect them. As **gravity** on the Moon is very weak, they bounced around instead of walking!

After two and a half hours of exploring the Moon and collecting rocks to bring back to Earth, the astronauts prepared for take-off in the lunar module. Then, they flew back to the command module to meet up with Michael Collins.

▼ The astronauts planted this US flag on the Moon as a sign that they had arrived there first. They had won the Space Race!

FIND OUT FOR YOURSELF
How many men have walked on the Moon in total?

<u>HOW</u> do we know?

We can see samples of the Moon rocks that the astronauts brought back to Earth in museums around the world, such as the Science Museum in London.

◄ A sample of rock from the Moon.

► The lunar module leaving the surface of the Moon.

BACK TO EARTH

Powerful **booster rockets** sent the command module back to Earth, with the three astronauts inside. It splash-landed in the ocean, where it floated on a rubber raft until people arrived to help the astronauts leave the spacecraft.

The *Apollo 11* crew were taken to an **airtight cabin**. They had to stay there for 18 days in case they had caught any dangerous diseases on the Moon.

▼ The command module was the only part of the *Apollo 11* spacecraft to return to Earth.

FIND OUT FOR YOURSELF
Which ocean did the astronauts land in?

The Moon landing had made the astronauts famous. Many important people spoke with them through the window of their cabin.

▼ The then president of the USA, Richard Nixon, came to visit the astronauts in their cabin.

WHAT do you think?

How do you think the astronauts felt after they arrived back on Earth?

HORNET + 3

Let us out!

AFTER APOLLO 11

After *Apollo 11*, there were five more *Apollo* landings on the Moon. Each *Apollo* mission had a different crew, and none of the *Apollo 11* crew members went into space again. As technology got better, NASA was able to do more experiments and learn more about the Moon.

FIND OUT FOR YOURSELF

When was the last *Apollo* landing on the Moon?

▼ The *Apollo 15* crew explored a large area of the Moon in a **rover**.

How fast can this thing go?!

Today, astronauts live in space on the **International Space Station**. Some astronauts are even considering living on other planets, such as Mars.

HOW do we know?

You can read about NASA's plans to travel to Mars online. Artists have drawn what **colonies** on other planets would look like.

WHAT do you think?

What would be difficult about life on the Moon or on planets such as Mars?

▲ Artists have drawn their ideas of what colonies on other planets might look like.

LIFE AFTER THE MOON LANDING

Neil Armstrong didn't like the **fame** that followed his landing on the Moon. He wanted a private life. He decided to leave NASA, and become a university professor, teaching other people how aircraft are made and flown.

Even though Armstrong was **out of the spotlight** until his death in August 2012, his bravery and skills as an astronaut were never forgotten. He will always be remembered as the first person to set foot on the Moon.

▶ Purdue University, where Armstrong studied, built this statue in his honour.

HOW do we know?

After Neil Armstrong's death, many important people wrote about their memories of him.

> 66 Neil was among the greatest of American heroes – not just of his time, but of all time. 99
>
> Barack Obama

Edwin (Buzz) Aldrin

Michael Collins

Neil Armstrong

Barack Obama

WHAT do you think?

Why will you remember Neil Armstrong?

▲ Neil Armstrong and the other *Apollo 11* crew members met Barack Obama, the then president of the USA, in 2009.

29

GLOSSARY

aircraft – a vehicle that can fly

airtight cabin – a closed space where no air can go in or come out

board – to get on to a vehicle

booster rockets – rockets that launch an object through space

broadcast – to transmit on TV and radio

colony – an area where people live together

command module – the part of the spacecraft that carries the astronauts through space

command pilot – the pilot who is in charge of a mission

experienced – describes someone who has skills and knowledge of something because they have done it many times

eyewitness – someone who sees an event happen

fame – being known by lots of people because of your actions

fighter plane – an aeroplane used during a war to drop bombs and attack other aeroplanes

gravity – the force that pulls objects to the ground

International Space Station – a space station in permanent orbit around the Earth where astronauts do experiments

interview – a meeting in which someone is asked questions

Korean War – a war in which the USA and South Korea fought against North Korea, the Soviet Union and China (1950–1953)

lunar module – the part of the spacecraft that lands on the Moon

manned – describes something that has a human crew

mission – a journey made by spacecraft

NASA – National Aeronautics and Space Administration. NASA is a US organisation that explores space.

orbit – to make a circular journey around a planet or a star

out of the spotlight – not in the newspapers or on TV

oxygen – a gas in the air that humans need to breathe to survive

rover – a vehicle used to explore the surface of other planets

service module – the part of the spacecraft that attaches to the rockets

Soviet Union – a former country in Asia and Europe. The Soviet Union broke up in 1991 and today it is divided into separate countries, such as Russia.

Space Race – the competition between the USA and the Soviet Union in the 1950s and 1960s, in which both countries tried to be the first to explore different areas of space

spacewalk – moving in space outside of a spacecraft

test pilot – someone who tests new aeroplanes as their job

Tranquility Base – the site where *Apollo 11* landed on the Moon

TIMELINE

1930 — Neil Armstrong is born.

1955 — Neil Armstrong starts working for NASA.

1961 — Yuri Gagarin becomes the first man in space.

1966 — Neil Armstrong travels into space for the first time on the *Gemini 8* flight.

1969 — Neil Armstrong takes the first steps on the Moon as part of the *Apollo 11* mission.

1971 — Neil Armstrong leaves NASA and becomes a university professor.

1978 — Neil Armstrong is given the Congressional Space Medal of Honor.

2012 — Neil Armstrong dies at the age of 82.

FIND OUT FOR YOURSELF ANSWERS

p7 – Wapakoneta
p9 – The Soviet Union/Russia
p17 – Michael Collins
p22 – Twelve
p24 – The Pacific Ocean
p26 – 1972

INDEX